Book Description

Tired of being stuck in a chair behind a desk?

Do you want to write more without sacrificing your health and sanity?

Learn how you can get more written while
- Hiking or just going for a stroll
- Driving
- Watching your kids play at the park
- Taking a bath

Multiple *New York Times* bestselling author Kevin J. Anderson has written 160 books—nearly fifteen million words!—most of them by dictating into a hand-held recorder while hiking.

Award-winning novelist and short story writer Martin L. Shoemaker dictates chapters and stories while driving, turning his daily commute into a productive work session.

These two die-hard "dictators" share their techniques and insights into how dictation can help you
- Improve your writing productivity

• Use otherwise lost time to brainstorm, plot, develop characters, write articles, and more

• Get inspired by leaving your confined office and getting a fresh perspective elsewhere

• Stay in shape while writing

On Being a Dictator, part of the Million Dollar Writing Series, will help you think outside the box, consider a different writing method, and up your game in the fast-paced ever-changing world of publishing.

ON BEING A DICTATOR

Using Dictation to Be a Better Writer

KEVIN J. ANDERSON
MARTIN L. SHOEMAKER

WFP
WORDFIRE PRESS

On Being a Dictator:
Using Dictation to Be a Better Writer

by Kevin J. Anderson
and Martin L. Shoemaker

EBook ISBN: 978-1-68057-020-5
Trade Paperback ISBN: 978-1-68057-018-2
Cover design by Janet McDonald
Art Director Kevin J. Anderson
Cover artwork images by Adobe Stock
Published by
WordFire Press LLC
PO Box 1840
Monument CO 80132
Kevin J. Anderson & Rebecca Moesta, Publishers
WordFire Press eBook Edition 2019
WordFire Press Trade Paperback Edition 2019
Printed in the USA

Join our WordFire Press Readers Group for
sneak previews, updates, new projects, and giveaways.
Sign up at wordfirepress.com

❀ Created with Vellum

Contents

The Million Dollar Writing Series

When seeking advice, always consider the source. Many self-appointed "experts" write how-to books without themselves ever accomplishing the thing they are trying to teach you how to do.

Each of the main authors in the Million Dollar Writing Series has sold a minimum of one million dollars of commercial product in their field. They have proved themselves, and here they share their wisdom, advice, and experience with you.

There are many factors in becoming a successful writer, and we cannot guarantee that you'll break into the top levels, but we hope you find the advice to be useful and enlightening.

Introduction:
Walking and Talking
KEVIN J. ANDERSON

Some people get their ideas in the shower. I do my best thinking when I'm out walking.

Strolling through a forest surrounded by beautiful scenery primes the pump in my imagination. Physical activity, walking along a trail or a bike path, frees me from distractions and lets the sentences flow. (Of course, there's also a literal separation from distractions if I'm on a long walk far from my office, because there's no ringing phone or doorbell, no obnoxious email alerts, no attention-hungry cats who do not understand writing deadlines.)

Very early in my career I discovered the effectiveness of taking a walk when I needed to mull over a storyline, brainstorm ideas with myself, get to know my characters as best friends instead of mere acquaintances. Wandering the streets around my home, strolling down the local bike path, or hiking on a nice trail always gave me inspiration.

Recent studies have pointed out what I've always known—that walking unlocks creativity, oils the wheels in your brain, and removes roadblocks to letting your ideas flow. Instead of including footnotes and a long list of academic-style references, I'll just ask you to Google "creativity and walking" and you'll find TED talks, Stanford University studies, *Psychology Today* articles, and more.

Taking a walk while trying to solve a plot problem or work out a character issue presented a serious problem, though: I'd often get so many ideas that I couldn't remember them all by the time I got back to my office. In one instance, I worked out the intricacies of a complicated climactic battle scene with multiple characters, each one having a requisite moment of glory or moment of tragedy, and I raced back home, trying to hold it all in my head. Alas, I forgot most of it by the time I got home.

After that disaster, I started carrying a small notebook in my pocket so that as the ideas came to me I could jot them down. But writing on a little spiral notebook while walking—especially if it's drizzling or snowing—is not the most convenient or efficient activity. I would often think up complete sentences, the perfect opening line or a full-fledged description of a character or place ... and I could never scribble it down quickly enough.

Finally, I tried taking a handheld microcassette recorder along on my walks. Whenever I thought of something good, I'd hit the Record button and say the words in my head, complete sentences, even complete paragraphs. I could preserve my thoughts as quickly as they came to me. Sometimes I would have a blizzard of ideas, and I'd talk in a breathless rush just to get them all down. And I did. I wrote character biographies; I outlined plot details; I blocked out massive scenes, beat by beat.

As my outlines grew more detailed, I added texture, snippets of dialog, even drafted entire scenes or conversations that were clear in my head. It didn't take long for that work to evolve into dictating a full-blown draft.

I decided I liked to do my chapters that way.

Writers usually do their work with butt in the chair and fingers on the keyboard, staring at the screen for hours on end. That doesn't work for me—at all. I am an avid hiker, and my recorder allowed me to write my day's word count while hiking in a national park. Also, by going far enough away from everybody else, I could get in a "zone"—walking alone inside my fictional world with my imaginary friends—and get lost in the story.

Sometimes too lost. Yes, I'll tell an embarrassing anecdote.

My microcassette recorder used ninety-minute cassettes, forty-five minutes on a side. I'd walk along dictating my story until I reached the end of the tape, at which point I'd pop out the tape and flip it over. A bothersome interruption, yes, but not a terrible one.

One time, I was hiking in the canyons of southern

Utah, writing an action-packed technothriller, part of the novel *Artifact*. I walked along, fully into the story as events built to a head. I dictated forty-five minutes, at which point I flipped the cassette over and kept going. The story was really exciting, heading toward the climax! All of the plot threads were reaching a grand finale. I kept walking, kept dictating.

I filled up the second forty-five minutes and reached the end of the tape. I was so deep in the story I didn't want to be interrupted. I popped open the recorder, flipped the tape over, slipped it back in, and dictated another twenty minutes before I came to an abrupt halt and realized that I had just recorded over my first twenty minutes of dictation.

My cry of dismay echoed up and down the canyons. I inserted a fresh cassette and tried to recapture the part that I had recorded over, but I was so furious at myself I had a hard time concentrating on the words.

Fortunately, I now use a digital recorder and I never run out of space.

Dictation is my primary method of writing. If I'm stuck typing a chapter in my chair in front of a screen, I feel trapped and restless. I want to be walking, talking to myself.

In this book my fellow dictator, Martin L. Shoemaker, and I lay out some of our strategies in how to use dictation as a writing tool, how to learn, what equipment to use, what pitfalls to avoid.

Try the technique, it really works! Dictation has increased my productivity by an order of magnitude. Once you figure it out, you'll be walking around and talking to yourself, too.

Introduction: It Gets Easier
MARTIN L. SHOEMAKER

I blame Karl Kolchak.

I'm Martin L. Shoemaker, and I am a confirmed dictator. And while there are lots of people who influenced me in this—particularly my co-author here, Kevin J. Anderson—Karl Kolchak was the first. He was the protagonist of the influential early '70s TV horror show, *The Night Stalker*. He was an investigative reporter who tracked down monsters, aliens, and robots; and to give the viewer insight into what was going through his head, the scriptwriters fell back upon a simple device: he narrated his thoughts into a Dictaphone.

Like many of my generation, I loved that show. So I sometimes get a grin as I sit here, driving through the countryside, dictating into a recorder that looks an awful lot like Karl's.

The idea of dictating your thoughts was hardly a new one when I started my writing career. At the Superstars Writing Seminars, organized by Kevin and his wife Rebecca Moesta, Kevin spoke several times about his dictation habits. My fellow writers and I discussed it now and then when we were looking for ways to find more writing time in our lives, but I always heard the same comments. "I tried it, and it didn't work." "I guess it might work for some people, but not for me." And the ever popular: "I hate the sound of my voice!"

I personally was in the "I guess it might work" camp, but I didn't try it until one day I totaled up the actual time I had available for writing. I'm a programmer, which is an absolutely rewarding job for me, but sometimes one with long hours. And I have responsibilities at home: meals to make, dishes to clean, the bird to feed, and more. And on top of all that, my commute to work is an hour each way. Even after giving up television and much of my reading, there just wasn't a lot of writing time for me to squeeze out of the day.

So I thought, why not try dictation? I figured it couldn't hurt, so I gave it a really serious try. And in that effort, stretched out over six weeks of commuting, I put together the second story that I sold to *Analog Science Fiction and Fact*: "Murder on the Aldrin Express." (To prove that dictation gets easier with practice ... "Murder on the Aldrin Express" was 19,000 words. I dictated the first draft of my novel, *Today I Am Carey*, in six weeks as well. That was 90,000 words.) So I guess it worked; but it was awkward and difficult, and it took me a lot of time to transcribe. (It was a mistake for me to transcribe manually, and it might be a mistake for you as well. We'll discuss that later.) I still didn't know if it was for me ...

Jump ahead four years, the year after I was a winner in the Writers of the Future contest (where I once again met Kevin and Rebecca and all of the other judges who are now my friends and peers). Along with some of my friends, I had been asked back to the workshop to talk to the new winners about how our careers had progressed since winning the contest. When it was my turn to talk, I discussed my Nebula-nominated short story, "Today I Am Paul." I explained how I had dictated that story in one drive to work, fifty minutes; and how, with only minor edits, I sent it out to get almost immediately accepted and published...and to win the Washington Science Fiction Association Small Press Award, and to appear in eight international translations. I mentioned that, looking back, every story I had sold in the past two years had been a dictated story.

I learn slowly, but even I heard what I said. Dictation was working for me. Maybe I should do it some more. Maybe it should become my normal way of writing.

And it has. Dictation has changed my productivity beyond belief. And when we had a similar discussion at the next year's workshop, I told people how well it was working for me; but I also realized that I had glossed over one point whenever I discussed dictation with other writers: it took me time to get so comfortable with dictation. It didn't happen overnight—it happened over years of learning, stumbling, and making mistakes. I found that I was unintentionally discouraging people: they thought I was some kind of freak (insert joke here) and dictation "just worked" for me; but it didn't work for them when they tried it. That was my mistake: not telling them that it didn't work for me at first, either. That there was a learning curve, but I got through it. And they could, too.

And you can, too.

And my hope is that in this volume, Kevin and I can help you to map out that learning curve. We can show you some of the mistakes we made along the way (leaving you to make new ones, of course) and help you to answer some questions before they come up. Dictation has changed my life as a writer. I believe it can change yours as well. Let us try to show you how.

Talking to Myself—Why Dictate?

If you see a person walking along engaged in a vigorous conversation with no one else around, it doesn't necessarily mean he's escaped from the nearest asylum. It could be me talking to myself. But don't be concerned, don't interrupt me, don't bother me at all —I'm writing.

It's been many years since I gave up the keyboard and took up a recorder for my first drafts. Since that time, I've dictated a hundred and fifty novels, speaking the words aloud, rather than typing them on a keyboard.

Maybe you're perfectly satisfied with sitting at your cramped card table after shoving aside the checkbook and the bills to clear a spot for writing. If you really work best that way, then I salute you. For me, as I write this chapter, I am hiking in a canyon above the Colorado River, making my way up to a pristine lake and a spectacular waterfall—I wouldn't trade places in a thousand years.

Let's look at some of the reasons why you should consider writing by dictation.

For Your Inspiration ...

One of the primary advantages of writing with a digital recorder is that you can do your work outside in a spectacular area, bombarded with inspiration. The world is my office and the details of nature or history itself can provide story fodder.

Under a tight deadline for one of my Star Wars novels, I went to Sequoia National Park, where I planned to isolate myself and get a lot of writing done. After I had settled into my cabin, a mountain snowstorm hit and made the roads impassable. The next day, I trudged out into the new-fallen snow, breaking trail among the pine trees and winding along cross-country ski paths to see frozen waterfalls and beautiful ice shelves on granite outcroppings.

While I walked, smelling the frosty air, seeing my breath in front of me and listening to the wind in the Sierra Nevada mountains, I wrote about Han Solo on the polar icecaps of an alien world. My cold and snowy "office" gave me perfect inspiration for writing that scene.

Other times I have hiked through the arid canyons of Death Valley, along dried ocean beds and over powdery sand dunes. While feeling the heat and the dry crackling air, I wrote many chapters in my Dune novels with Brian Herbert. What could possibly be a better office for writing the story of a waterless planet that would make the Sahara seem like an oasis?

I spent a week in Capital Reef National Park in the slickrock canyons of southern Utah, where I wrote many chapters in my Saga of Seven Suns novels. During my daily hikes, I dictated the adventures of characters exploring ancient, abandoned cities within rock overhangs, very similar to the Anasazi ruins I visited in person.

Even if you aren't in a place relevant to your subject matter, you can still experience sounds and smells and sensations that add vivid details to your prose—details you may not remember while sitting numbed in your cluttered office at home.

For Your Health ...

Another advantage of dictating while out walking is the solitude and the peace-of-mind you'll encounter. While hiking, you can let your mind sink into the universe of your story, blessedly without interruptions. Out on the trail with your digital recorder, you can avoid telephone calls (because you have wisely turned off your cell phone), social media, the temptation to read your email, do the dishes, scrub the toilets, clean the attic ...

Let's face it, writing is a sedentary profession. Full-time authors spend their days seated in front of a screen without a great deal of exercise. Personally, I hate being cooped up in the office and would rather be hiking, or even just walking along bike paths in an urban area. Once I learned how to dictate, I no longer had to choose between a day of hiking or a day of writing. Now I can do both at the same time. Dictation keeps me fit and active.

On a more serious note, some writers are medically forced to abandon the keyboard and have to choose between giving up writing altogether or finding a different method. My wife, bestselling author Rebecca Moesta, suffered from severe carpal tunnel syndrome in both wrists and cubital tunnel nerve entrapment in both elbows, which in the end cost her four surgeries and a draconian reduction of her keyboard time.

Rebecca had always considered me somewhat eccentric with my technique of dictating, but now she found herself forced to get a headset and recorder of her own (though she chooses to spend her dictating time on a treadmill or in a shopping mall, rather than out on a forest trail).

For Your Productivity ...

When I'm dictating I manage to produce far more pages in less time than if I'm chained to my desk. I've even learned how to fool myself into writing more than I originally intended to do. In a trick I call the "round-trip deception," I will keep hiking outbound until I have completed one entire chapter ... at which point I should have just enough time on the way back to dictate another full chapter. Since I have to walk back anyway, I might as well be writing.

During the week I recently spent in southern Utah, I hiked a total of fifty miles and wrote 168 pages in my new novel, as well as this article. (Hmmm, that's about three-and-a-half pages per mile!)

It would have been impossible for me to do this much at home with numerous distractions.

And the Drawbacks ...

The most obvious drawback with dictation is that once you've recorded a chapter, then it must be transcribed. Depending on how fast you type, you can transcribe your own files, of course—but to me this defeats the purpose of using a recorder. In the time it takes to transcribe a chapter, I could just as well have written a completely new one.

But it's not an insurmountable obstacle. See Chapter 9 below about typists, transcription services, and transcription software.

For Your Consideration ...

Always keep in mind that, like any other writing technique, dictation is a skill that must be learned. Give it time and practice.

You may become self-conscious when people look at you talking surreptitiously into your digital recorder —but, in the words of Richard Feynman, "What do you care what people think?" I'm walking along involved in a story, writing what just might become a best-selling novel. Other people probably assume you're talking on a Bluetooth set.

So keep an open mind if you are willing to try a new writing technique. Go out and talk to yourself.

—KJA

2

"I Just Can't Write That Way" and Other Myths

I know what you're going to say. I've been proselytizing about writing by dictation for long enough that I've seen the initial reactions, the looks of bewilderment, the heads shaking, the heels digging in.

"I just can't write that way," or "It doesn't feel natural."

Well, I call BS.

Fiction is a verbal art. From the dawn of time, storytellers were sitting around the campfire, spinning out the yarn of a spectacular mammoth hunt or describing legends of their gods and heroes. Even today, what fisherman hasn't talked at length about the one that got away? When you're writing a novel, you are just creating an even bigger fish tale. Writers like to tell stories. It's how our brains work.

"I tried it once, but it just didn't work for me."

Like everything else, writing by dictation is a learned skill, something that requires practice. As you learn to think and write by dictation, it will get easier and you will get faster, more adept.

Consider the first time you sat in front of a keyboard. Did you instantly know how to type? Were you knocking out ninety words a minute? No. You had to learn how to type. Your brain and your fingers gradually got accustomed to where the keys were and how to form words.

Dictation is similar. Once you practice writing this way, and keep practicing, you get better at it. Writing by speaking aloud begins to feel more natural (or it returns to being natural) once you realize that you don't have to type your sentences.

"I feel awkward. People are staring at me!"

I can sympathize. When I started dictating, it truly was an unusual thing. I would walk along holding a device up to my mouth and muttering about dragons or space stations. This was long before ubiquitous cell phones and Bluetooth headsets. People would look at me like an oddball talking to voices in my head. I was indeed in an imaginary world of my own, spouting out character dialogue and describing alien worlds. But I was at work!

That's why I liked to write while hiking, off on a trail deep in the wilderness. Alone. The squirrels didn't really care what I was doing.

Today, however, that stigma is gone. Everyone wanders around talking to themselves, pressing a phone up against their face or talking into a headset. No one even notices. You don't have to feel self-conscious. Just get into the zone and read out loud the sentences that appear in your head.

"I just can't write that way. It's not natural."

Most writers have been typing their prose on a keyboard and reading it on the screen for so long, it's hard for them to consider any other way of writing.

But ... really? Dictation is not natural? Think about that and go through the detailed process in your head. If you're typing on a keyboard, you think up a sentence in your mind, then your brain breaks down that sentence into separate words, and then those words into individual letters. Next, your brain sends a signal to your fingers to find those particular letters on a randomly arranged keyboard, which reproduces the letters, to make the words, to make the sentence, which then appears on your screen. (Remember, the QWERTY keyboard was intentionally designed to slow down typists!)

When dictating, though, you think up the sentence and speak it out loud. That's it, two steps. Straight from brain to the recorder.

Typing prose on a keyboard is by no means more "natural" than dictating it. You just have to make a paradigm shift.

—KJA

I would add one more common objection: "I hate the sound of my voice!"

This is just another form of "I feel awk–ward." Do you really hate the sound of your voice? Or do you hate the awkward experience? If it's the latter, Kevin addresses awkwardness above.

Still, I'll concede that many people who aren't in the speaking or singing business hate the sound of their voice. There are reasons for this, both physical (your voice in your own head has resonance that it doesn't have outside your skull) and psychological (it's creepy to hear yourself speaking from somewhere else).

But you can get over that. Singers, actors, and teachers do. And you don't need fancy voice training for it, you just have to get used to the experience. If most people think their own voice sounds weird, and yet most voices don't sound weird to you, then over time you discover that this is normal. Your voice is fine.

Besides, as we will encourage you throughout this book, it won't be you listening to your recorded voice. It will be a transcriptionist or transcription software. Believe me, the transcriptionist doesn't care. The software can't care. You can dictate without worry. Your voice is fine.

—MLS

3

Use Cases for Dictation

In software development, we have the concept we call a "use case": a description of how a specific user will use your system to perform a particular task in order to accomplish a particular goal. If a different user had different goals, that might be another use case. If your user had a different task to accomplish, that might be another use case. If your time or schedule or budget meant you had to change the way you work, that would be another use case. So as a programmer, when I think of solving problems, I think of use cases.

Dictation has use cases as well. And your use cases are going to determine your best options when it comes to dictation. For instance, my use case can be summarized as follows:

Martin wants to write lots of words, but he has an hour commute each way to and from work, taking two hours out of his day. That's on top of the eight to ten hours that the work can take. He also has to sleep and take care of family matters around the home; and he has to conduct the business side of writing. He needs more hours in his day, so he wants to turn his two hours of commute into two hours of writing time, which can produce anywhere from 3,000 to 10,000 words per day. That can produce a novel in a month, which has a lot of value for him. He needs a way that he can safely dictate while driving. He must not have to look at a device nor tap the screen. He must be able to dictate hands-free, touching controls only when the vehicle is stopped. And because stops might be short, such as at a traffic light or stop sign, they should be controls which he can easily find by touch. For this reason, Martin does not use a recorder app that's available for a modest price on his phone, nor does he use the Bluetooth headset that connects to his phone. He uses a Sennheiser ME-3 cardioid microphone plugged into an Olympus handheld recorder which is then plugged into his Jeep's audio system so that he can hear the results and not worry that the recording might have spontaneously stopped (as can happen with some recording applications on his phone).

I'll talk more about my process later, but that's a pretty good summary of my use case for dictation. Your use case might be different. You might be Kevin, hiking through the Rockies. So maybe a phone might work better for him. (Or maybe not: I know he chooses a handheld device, a higher-end model than mine.) He might want a headset microphone, or he might be satisfied with the microphone built into his recorder.

Your use case might be that you want to sit in your

quiet office and talk to yourself. In that case, your best option might be dictating directly into the computer, if you have a high-end soundboard that does high-fidelity recording.

Your use case might be that of the late Sir Terry Pratchett, who in his later years suffered from Alzheimer's disease and could no longer reliably type. He switched to dictation so that he could dictate, and so he used Dragon NaturallySpeaking's advanced features to edit by voice. That's a different use case.

So when Kevin talks about his process or I talk about mine, keep in mind that these are processes fitted to our specific use cases. We will try to discuss other use cases we know of, other practices we have heard of or experimented with; but you may have to adapt these to your particular constraints and goals.

Think about your use cases. Do you need to be hands-free? Do you need to be eyes-free? Do you need to be mobile? Do you need to be in your quiet office? Will you be dictating in a noisy environment? Will you be paying a service to do your transcription, or will you be using software?

There are a lot of questions you'll have to answer; but you don't have to answer them all right away. We're going to raise some of them for you, and you should think about them. But your answers will change as you learn.

—MLS

4

Baby Steps—Getting Started with Dictation

New "dictators" often stumble by thinking that they have to start out dictating perfect finished prose, as if they are reading an audiobook of the novel in their head. After three decades of practice and—no kidding —fifteen million words or more, I can dictate a pretty clean first draft.

But I didn't start out that way, and neither should you. There are many aspects to using dictation as a creative tool. Let's start out with baby steps. Try a few exercises that may seem easier, more useful, and not so intimidating than writing finished prose.

First, think about doing dictation just for yourself, the equivalent of notes, rough drafts, sketches—things that no one needs to see but you. Use your recording device (see Chapter 8) as a way to capture your thoughts.

I work on massive novels, often over 180,000 words, with dozens of characters and storylines, usually part of an extended series. When I'm just starting work on a book, sketching out the broad strokes and putting all the pieces together, I have an overall picture in my mind, but none of the details.

At this stage, when all the storylines are up for grabs, I like to take long walks while keeping the recorder handy. I let my imagination flow, spouting out ideas. This character could go to that alien planet and have such-and-such adventure. What if there's a conflict between Character B and Character N? Remember to find the artifact we established in Book 2. Start a romance between character A and character B. This scene has to occur before that event in order to set up this plot twist. (It makes more sense when I can use specifics.)

When you walk along and dictate these ideas, you don't have to be grammatically correct. No one else will listen to them or read your words. These are just notes for you. Understanding that your dictation doesn't have to be perfect should take away some of the self-conscious concerns.

I use dictation when I'm choreographing big battle scenes or climactic events where multiple storylines come together, dozens of characters clash and either kill each other or rescue each other. In order for it all to be worked out, these events have to be mapped thoroughly, the storylines braided and organized like the sheet music for an entire symphony, and I am the conductor. I use dictation to map out scenes and put things in order as they occur to me. These building blocks are just in a jumble, to be organized later.

Another beginner step is to do character sketches,

flesh out biographies and backgrounds of the people in the story. When developing a novel from scratch, I'll go for a drive or walk and just get into the heads of the main characters, one at a time, like an actor taking on a role. How old is she? What is her hair color and how does she wear it? What sorts of clothes does she prefer—glitzy and formal, scruffy and casual? Does she have brothers and sisters? What was their interaction as children? How is her home life? What kind of music does she like? What was her first romance?

As I ask questions about the character, I'll come up with anecdotes that help build her back story. Let's consider Millicent, the female lead in a new young adult fantasy. Think of a time when she got lost in the castle catacombs looking for her kitten, and thereby accidentally discovered long-forgotten tunnels where she can hide later on in the story when the trolls capture the castle. Or a pleasant memory of how she helped in the castle kitchens making Christmas pastries, but she got scared when she found a rat behind the flour bins. How she got a terrible fever when she was young and thought she was going to die. She remembers how she lay shivering, sweating, barely holding on … and her favorite aunt tended her, bathed her forehead, fed her broth, and spent so much time next to her that the aunt also caught the fever and died, leaving the poor girl with sweet memories and a lot of guilt.

These little things come to me as I walk and ponder, and they will be added to the finished book. None of this has to be in order. It's a free association, a brainstorming session, but you focus your thoughts and forget about the recorder in your hand, your mind is directed towards developing Millicent.

By shutting out all the other distractions and just putting on your new character costume, then walking a mile in their shoes, you'll end up with a far greater understanding of their personality and history.

Again, none of this needs to be deathless prose. You don't even have to transcribe the file, because you've preserved your words in the recording itself. But the mere process of dictating it, brainstorming it aloud, gives your thoughts a structure and a permanence beyond what you would achieve by silently mulling over the thoughts in your head and hoping you don't forget the details.

Using dictation for notes and brainstorming is a perfect first step, without worrying about finished text. Try the baby steps. Get proficient at dictating ideas, and soon you'll get comfortable enough to dictate actual sentences or paragraphs.

Even if you never progress beyond this step, it's not a mere stepping stone. I still use my recorder as one of my best tools for brainstorming.

—KJA

I would add a very mercenary perspective: these notes and sketches can serve as the basis for other stories, perhaps short stories set in the world of your larger work. You can then sell these to short fiction

KEVIN J. ANDERSON & MARTIN L. SHOEMAKER

markets, publish them in collections, or even give them away to promote a novel.

If you build a successful series, readers always want to know more about your world, and these notes give you a ready source to meet that demand. If your work becomes popular enough, like Dune or The Lord of the Rings, readers will want to read everything: maps, concordances, timelines, family trees …

You can't control whether this will happen, but if you have an archive of dictated notes, you'll be ready if it does.

—MLS

5

Dictating Finished Prose

Now that you're proficient with brainstorming and dictating notes, it's time to start speaking finished sentences and paragraphs—you know, actually writing by dictation.

If you're a pantser—writing your stories or entire novels by the seat of your pants and seeing where it goes—the method is clear: just start walking or driving, and go for it! Martin has a whole chapter about that next.

I have always been a plotter, even a militant plotter. Most of my novels are giant intricate epics with multiple interconnected plotlines and numerous point-of-view characters. Getting the novel to come together is like herding cats, and it doesn't just happen by accident. An architect constructing a massive hotel doesn't just start digging holes and putting up walls willy-nilly. She draws a detailed blueprint first.

Thus, I write very clear and specific outlines,

chapter by chapter. I find it an invaluable aid with my dictation.

Right now, I am writing the second epic fantasy novel in my Wake the Dragon series, called *Vengewar*, which will have 100 chapters. (I know, because I outlined.) As I prepare to start writing, I outline those hundred chapters, character by character, scene by scene. For each chapter, I write a brief description, a paragraph long. This lays down the chapter's point-of-view and the key event that has to happen, the beginning, and where it ends, leading into the next chapter. This lets me identify how this particular chapter moves the plot forward, the main action, and what changes from beginning to end. Every chapter should be like a separate short story with an arc, a primary scene, dialogue and description.

Each day as I go out for a walk, I write two chapters on average. I print out the descriptions of those chapters and carry the notes with me. If it's a more extensive hike, I'll take three or four chapter descriptions.

I go out walking, paper in hand for reference, but then I slip into my zone, walking along and fleshing out all of the events in my short description, occasionally referring to the notes. It's like taking the movie trailer and turning it into the full movie.

For instance, here's a chapter I wrote just a few days ago.

Chapter 46: Mandan and Utho with their ten Commonwealth warships as they attack the 17

Isharan vessels defending Fulcor Island. It's a devastating naval battle. The new rulers of Fulcor have built siege engines that launch magical chemical fire upon the Commonwealth ships. Mandan panics and calls a retreat although Utho thinks they should stay and keep fighting. Nevertheless, he protects Mandan, and the Commonwealth fleet retreats, humiliated. Fleeing, they sail around the island, and two ships run onto the hidden reefs and sink. It's a devastating defeat.

Those few sentences about the attack and then the humiliating defeat don't tell the whole story. Is reading the score of the Super Bowl the same as watching the game? When I dictated that chapter, I fleshed out those 86 words from the outline into 2,700 words, nine pages.

Many writers will argue about plotting versus pantsing. (In fact, Martin and I argue about it! See the next chapter.) Pantsers complain there's no creativity if an author rigidly outlines ahead of time. As you can see from the example above, even though I plot my chapters in a novel very carefully, there's plenty of room to move within each chapter.

Every time I go out walking, I unleash my inner pantser. Yes, in Chapter 46 of *Vengewar*, I know there has to be a naval battle, the Commonwealth ships versus enemy vessels around Fulcor Island, and the battle is a disaster, with several ships wrecked on the reefs or destroyed by catapult fire.

But how exactly does it happen? How do you lay

out big events? What are the details that make it come alive? That's where the creative freedom comes from for each chapter.

As I walk along, I think about the scene, picture the events, imagine the point of view, fashion the dialogue—just the way any writer does when typing on a keyboard, except I speak my sentences out loud.

Once transcribed, some of these sentences may be rough or grammatically incorrect. Words may be redundant. Just remember this is draft prose. I don't know many writers who can (or should!) publish their first-draft prose. It all requires editing. When my transcribed file comes back from the typist, I go over the draft, clean up the punctuation, edit the sloppy prose. Keep in mind that it would be sloppy prose if I typed it on a keyboard, as well. My novels generally go through six drafts before I consider them ready for publication.

In the appendix to this book, I have included the brief chapter description for the opening of my vampire thriller novel *Stake*, plus the Word file as it came back from the typist—therefore, exactly the words I dictated (while driving, in this case). Following that, I've attached the final polished version so you can see all the steps. You can even listen to the original audio file at https://myaudiosample.com/dictator and hear the words as I spoke them.

This way you can walk along in my shoes as I create a new chapter.

—KJA

6

Dictating for Pantsers:
The Instant Story Show

Kevin has explained some best practices for dictation that will let you plan and prepare what you're going to dictate, so that you're ready to go as soon as you sit down and start talking. That's some excellent advice; and now I'm going to tell you how to ignore all of it.

If you spend much time among other writers, you're no doubt familiar with the dichotomy between plotters and pantsers. Plotters meticulously plan out what the story is supposed to be so that they have a path to follow and don't get lost along the way. The outline is not iron shackles: they can veer from it when they find the story needs to. Some will only plot a little ways ahead, and then re-plot as they go. Others will make elaborate outlines, running into many pages. Plotters want to know where they're going, giving them confidence in what they're going to produce. They find that this lets them produce their work quickly.

Pantsers say, "What fun is that?" They enjoy the

surprise of the story as they write. This is sometimes called discovery writing. And this is where my sympathies lie. I sometimes have vague, shadowy hints of where the story is going, but I'm far more often surprised (especially on short stories—I plot a little more carefully for novels).

Probably the best story I have ever written, "Today I Am Paul," started with a simple premise and an opening line that I had in my morning shower. That gave me ideas of what the story was about, but no idea where it was going. I finished my shower and got ready for work as quickly as I could. I sat down in my Jeep, and I started dictating.

Fifty minutes later I was at work and I had 5,000 words dictated. I sent it off to my first readers, and they told me that it was a wonderful story with an almost wonderful ending, but my last two paragraphs were weak.

By that time, I'd had two days to think about it. I read it, decided they were right, replaced those two with three better paragraphs, and sent it off to *Clarkesworld Magazine*. Neil Clarke bought it, and it went on to a Nebula nomination, a Small Press Award, four *Year's Best* appearances, and eight international editions. And I had no idea where the story was going when I sat down to dictate it. So yeah, I'm a pantser, confirmed.

So how do you dictate with absolutely no idea where you're going? Well, Dean Wesley Smith, a confirmed pantser as well, teaches a workshop on openings. These ideas aren't original with him; I've heard them from other writers as well. They go back a long way.

The key to a good opening in this approach is three elements: a character, in a setting, with a problem. It might not be the problem that the story revolves around, but it's a problem that engages that character. And thus it engages the reader, because while attacking the problem, the character is revealed and the setting is explored. This is enough to pull the reader into the story.

And as a confirmed pantser, this is enough to get me going. Will I find a good story at the end of it? Maybe. Maybe not. More often than not, I do; but on the days that I don't, I simply attribute that to practice. That's a dirty little word that some writers seem to think we're not supposed to do. Other artists, in music or painting or dance, are expected to rehearse and practice and produce studies, all to master their techniques and understand how to work better. But writers talk of "wasting words." Balderdash! Words aren't wasted, but sometimes they're just practice.

So I will often sit down in my Jeep, think of a character and a setting and a problem, and just start dictating; and sometimes these are my best stories. I might have a little idea that came up in the shower that morning … "An android taking care of an Alzheimer's patient by pretending to be her absent family." "A murder mystery on a Mars cycler." "An ex-soldier recovering bodies lost on distant planets." But mostly I just sit down and start dictating.

This has become so comfortable for me now that I

have started performing the Instant Story Show at science fiction conventions. This is basically improv for writers. I ask the audience for my character and my setting and my problem; and for the next fifty minutes or so, I dictate a story live before their eyes. If I find myself stammering and at a loss, I have them draw a card from a special deck and read a random story element to get me going again. By the end of an hour, I usually have a story that's finished and ready to go. After the session, I pull it into Dragon Naturally-Speaking to transcribe it, I edit it, and I put it up on Kindle. It's often ready to purchase by the end of the convention.

Are these great stories? Eh. They're good ones, more often than not. Occasionally even great. The audience sure enjoys the show (though I think they enjoy watching me stumble just as much as they enjoy the process). So far, none have been stories that have embarrassed me. They've all been good enough. And as my mentor Mike Resnick says, they can't all be your best work.

So if you're a pantser, don't despair. Dictation is for you, too.

—MLS

7

Ride Along: Dictating While Driving

Rather than just explain my process of dictation, I'm going to actually do the process and describe to you what's happening as I do it. (Full disclosure: I've edited this at the keyboard after I dictated it.)

I do most of my dictation while driving to and from work. That's two hours out of my day that I can lose, or I can devote the time to writing. I have chosen to do the latter. On an average day I can get fifty words per minute while dictating. Even on a poor day I get around twenty-five; while on my best day, I get around one hundred. Let's go with twenty-five. Sixty minutes each way means one hundred-twenty minutes round trip, which means 3,000 words per day minimum. That ain't bad!

To start my day, I sit down in the Aldrin Express (my Jeep Liberty), I plug my voice recorder into my Jeep's audio, and I plug in the microphone. I plug into the audio because that way I can hear the recording as I'm making it, which allows me to detect if there are noise problems: interference, static, poor connections, feedback, etc. The worst, most disappointing thing is to dictate a really great hour of text only to find that it's unintelligible. If there are problems, I want to hear them as they happen.

Next, if I'm working on an ongoing project, I play back the last five minutes from the day before. This allows me to remember where I was. I call it seating myself in the story.

Once I've got myself seated, then I do a quick microphone check: a brief recording, ten seconds, just to check the sound quality. I play that back and verify that there are no problems, or I fix any that I find. Then I'm ready to go.

I start the recorder again, I put the Aldrin into gear, and I start driving. I pull down the little wooded driveway that leads to my narrow country road, and by the time I hit the turn signal, my brain is into the story. Or in today's case, into this chapter. I pull onto the short stretch of road, I hit the corner, and I'm off and running. Running at the mouth, that is.

Now you may wonder: is this a distraction when you're driving? And that's a very important question. Safety first! It does me no good to end up in the hospital. They don't like to have me dictating there; it annoys the other patients. So if I want to dictate on the road, I have to actually pay attention to the road.

But at least for me, talking to you on this recorder is no more distracting than if I were talking to you as a passenger in the Jeep. So come on, ride along with me. I'll explain a little more.

I'm still watching the road, still checking my turn signals, braking for things that look like road hazards, watching the speed limit, all the things you do when you're driving. I'm just carrying on a conversation at the same time. If I weren't dictating, I would be listening to an audiobook or to music. Or talking to myself, most likely, even if I weren't recording.

My brain can't sit still and just concentrate on the road. That makes me nervous. I'm a writer! I can imagine all sorts of things that might go wrong. Places where the deer might leap out. (We get those a lot in Michigan; I've hit seven in my driving career.) Places where the road might be flooded. Places where an alien invasion might come from out of nowhere and start blasting the road. All right, that last one hasn't happened yet; but if it does, I'll be sure to turn it into a story.

So I contend that I am not in actuality distracted. Your mileage will vary. (Get it? Mileage? While driving? All right, I'm sorry …) But there are two definitions of distraction: practical distraction and legal distraction; and a lot of my process is built around making sure that I am not legally distracted. Should I find myself stopped by an officer, I want to be able to say truthfully and in a court of law that I was not a distracted driver.

That brings up two points, the first easy, the second complex. The easy one is hearing. In many jurisdictions—I am not a lawyer, check your own laws, but this is the safe way to bet—it is illegal to have your ears covered while driving. You must be able to hear any warning sounds around you. So you need a microphone which does not include earphones. That shouldn't be hard to find, but it's something to consider when you're shopping. (See the following chapter.) I use a Sennheiser ME-3, which is over-the-ear for placement, but doesn't have earphones and doesn't cover the ears. It has a band that runs behind my head and over my ears to stabilize the boom mic in front of my face.

The other, more important element of distraction —both legal and practical—is hands-free operation. You want both hands on the wheel whenever possible. In many jurisdictions, it is illegal to be looking at an electronic device while driving. And it's always risky!

So your recording solution needs to be something you can operate without looking at it, and ideally without touching it. Or if you must touch it, it should have a few simple buttons which you can find by touch while keeping your hands mostly on the wheel. You will note that I started my recorder before I put the Aldrin into gear. I will stop it only when the vehicle is pulled to a halt, so that I do not hit that pedestrian who was just walking down the road beside me. (Hitting pedestrians is not a good plan.) Make sure that you're safely dictating while driving. If you don't have safety, don't dictate behind the wheel.

Now that safety matters are out of the way, let's talk about the process. Today, as most days, I am dictating in a linear order. Once in a while I realize I missed something, and I'll dictate myself a note. Note: go back and insert the thing I forgot, or change the thing that I got wrong. But for the most part, I am dictating in the order you are reading this. I will also sometimes record the same sentence more than once. I will also sometimes record the same sentence multiple times. I will also sometimes record the same sentence over and over until I find the version that I'm happy with, and then I keep that version in editing. With dictation, it's all about the editing. You clean it up when you can stop and look at it, but don't worry about perfection while you're dictating. I discussed that above in Chapter 3, but that's my process: get it done now, get it right later.

And that attitude of "Dictate now, edit later" also allows me to dictate in a nonlinear fashion, if that's the order the ideas come to me. My first dictated story, "Murder on the Aldrin Express," came to me in bits and pieces of dialogue and scene setting over the course of several weeks of driving to and from work. Dictation was a brand new experience for me, and I was learning as I went, so I didn't really have a method yet. I was just determined to turn those two hours per day into something useful.

I have to say it worked. I wrote that story specifically for *Analog Science Fiction and Fact*, in what I hoped would be my second sale to them; and sure enough, Stan Schmidt bought it, one of his last acquisitions as Editor before Trevor Quachri took over his job. When the story came out, I got compliments from other professional writers, people I respected, and eventually Gardner Dozois purchased it for his *Year's Best Science Fiction, Thirty-First Annual Collection*. So with a start like that, you can understand why I'm a fan of dictation. If you dictate out of order, there's absolutely nothing wrong with that. Just get the thoughts out there; you can clean them up later.

So linear, nonlinear, whatever process works for you. Dictate your thoughts and keep going. One of the key benefits of dictation is you're making time productive that might not otherwise be.

That's all I can explain about my process of dictating while driving. It's really that simple. But that's only half the process. Once you've dictated, you have to turn that into printed text. We'll discuss transcription services and software in Chapter 9.

—MLS

Though I've talked mostly about writing while hiking, I also dictate as I drive in the car, though perhaps in a more reckless fashion than Martin, since I go "commando," holding the recorder in one hand while driving.

If I take a long trip, endless miles down a perfectly straight Interstate, it's easy to concentrate on my story and dictate many chapters on an hours-long excursion.

I've discovered the magic of productivity by dictating on even short drives, however. Two years ago, while teaching (and learning) at a Master Class workshop on the Oregon coast, I had to drive two miles from the hotel every morning to get our Starbucks. With traffic and stop lights, it was usually fifteen minutes each way. Inspired and determined to be more productive after several days of the intense class, I realized that even the roundtrip to Starbucks was useful time. I had agreed to write the introduction to a new science fiction anthology, only a thousand words or so. I knew what I wanted to say, and it didn't require great depths of planning or outlining. I dictated the complete introduction in two mornings of coffee runs—and I received $150 for it, more than enough to pay for Starbucks!

On short drives, I also dictate blogs, articles, as well as my sections in this book. Even fifteen minutes is enough to get something written.

—KJA

8

Equipment for the Road

As we've discussed above, there are many different reasons for choosing dictation; and your reasons will affect your choice of equipment.

As I noted, my primary reason for dictation is to turn my two hours of daily commute into two hours of writing time. That means that my overriding concern has to be safety. One hospital stay can really ruin my productivity.

A secondary concern is that my recordings are made in a ten-year-old Jeep driving 70 mph down a rural highway, sometimes with wind or rain or fans adding to the noise environment. I need equipment that will produce an intelligible recording despite the noise. Since it's impractical to have my computer there during my dictation, I need equipment that will record audio files for later transcription. (Other users may be dictating straight into their computer in a comfortable, quiet office.) And because I sometimes drive through zones with little or no cell phone service, I can't rely on equipment that needs an internet connection.

Again, these are my constraints, maybe not yours. They lead me to rule out some otherwise viable choices:

- Some of the most powerful transcription tools run only on a computer, not on a smaller device like a phone or a voice recorder; but driving and trying to use my computer at the same time is a really bad idea. I save the computer for later in my writing process. (If you plan to dictate in the comfort of your home or office, a computer with a good sound card may be a great choice.)
- There are various iPhone-based solutions I have tested (and also Android equivalents). Some of these have impressive transcription accuracy, using only the Bluetooth microphone that I use for telephone calls. And all of them attain that accuracy by delegating the transcription to a powerful server somewhere on the internet. Because my internet connection is intermittent, I cannot use these solutions. (If you plan to dictate only in areas with good internet connection, your cell phone and a good microphone may be a great choice. I'll discuss this more in the chapter on software later in the book.)

- Another problem with phone-based solutions is that a phone is not hands-free —at least not for these apps. The apps require me to look at a screen, find a spot on that screen, and tap that spot that feels exactly the same as every other spot on that smooth glass screen. That means I need at least two eyes, and one or maybe two hands. By contrast, I can operate a dedicated recorder with physical buttons while stopped at a traffic light, moving only one hand from the wheel long enough to feel the buttons. A phone-based solution won't work for me. (On the other hand ... I used to have a Windows Phone with an app called Rapid Recorder which I could control entirely by my Bluetooth earpiece and my voice, and which required no internet connection. If I could find the same features in an iPhone app, I might change my equipment choices.)

- As I discussed above when I described my dictation process, in many jurisdictions it's illegal to have both ears covered while driving. This rules out some otherwise excellent microphones because they're attached to full headsets. (If you don't plan to dictate and drive, you might prefer a microphone with a headset that cuts out external sound.)

- I also tried and rejected some nice low-cost

microphones that work well in a quiet environment but not in the noisy environment of my Jeep.

So given those choices that I didn't make, here's my transcription equipment:

- A Sennheiser ME 3-II headmic with cardioid capsule. This microphone has a metal frame that fits over your ears for stability but does not block your hearing. The frame anchors the adjustable microphone head in front of your mouth. The microphone has what they call a cardioid pickup pattern, meaning sound in one direction is amplified while sound in other directions is reduced or eliminated. If I wore the mic and we had a conversation, the mic would pick up only my voice—perhaps even if you shouted! I have dictated a story while sitting fifty yards from a concert, and none of the music could be heard in the recording. So this microphone is more than sufficient for eliminating road and traffic noise as I dictate. (I learned about the Sennheiser ME 3-II from the support forum at KnowBrainer.com, a company that sells speech-recognition hardware and software.)
- An Olympus Digital Voice Recorder WS-

853. This satisfies my requirements for physical, tactile buttons. (As a bonus, the recorder makes sounds when the buttons are pushed, so I don't have to guess.) It also has a USB plug, allowing me to easily copy files to my computer (and to recharge the battery); and it has an audio output jack, allowing me to plug it into the AUX port of my Jeep's stereo so I can listen as I dictate.

Again, these are the choices that work well for me, and the questions and answers that led me to choose them. I hope that I have given you questions to ask, so that you may make the best choices for your needs.

—MLS

For my setup, I use a hand-held Olympus digital recorder. Since I'm walking and talking, I just hold the thing and talk into it. Nothing as fancy as Martin's!

One "feature" you want to beware of is Voice Activated Recording—where the recorder senses your voice and automatically starts recording. It may sound convenient and better for hands-free operation, but the problem is that it always cuts off the first word or two of your sentence because it doesn't have instantaneous activation. No thanks. I'll just turn it on when I want to record.

Another detail to watch for: some sleek models have smooth, simple touch-activated buttons. In winter, I often use the recorder while wearing gloves. I need to be able to tell if I've pushed the button or not, so I need to have a real analog slider switch or click button. It has to be tactile so I know when it's actually on and recording, and when I have shut it off.

You can wear a head-mounted microphone, with a manual switch to turn it on or off (see the perils of voice-activated recording, above). Good recorders will have protected built-in microphones to cut down on wind noise, but you may also want to consider a wind-baffle for the microphone.

For years I used an Olympus DS-7000, which was a real workhorse. I loved it. It had a capacity to hold the dictation files for four to five complete novels (and I write long novels). The Olympus DSS software no longer supports the model, though, and I was forced to upgrade to the latest model, which includes count-less unnecessary, complex, and unwanted features that make walking and talking far less straightforward.

But I'm getting used to it, and writing at full speed.

—KJA

9

Transcribing Your Dictation

Typists and Transcription Services

Once you've dictated your story or chapter, now what do you do with your words? The dictation file doesn't do you any good as a writer unless you're going to stand in a room and play it aloud for an audience. (Yes, I have done that once or twice, but it's not a practical way to get a large readership.)

If you have a brief file or just some notes, you might decide to do the typing yourself. You might even bite the bullet and transcribe all of your chapters. But even though I, myself, am a fairly fast typist, I have no particular desire to transcribe an entire 180,000-word novel after I've dictated it. I have always considered the time transcribing to be better spent writing new material. Other people are able to do the typing. Only I can do the original writing.

So I needed a better way. I hired a typist.

At first, I used a coworker, someone who wanted to

pick up a little extra work. This was in the days of microcassettes, so I would physically deliver the small tapes one at a time every day after I had dictated my chapters. I felt a little like a spy surreptitiously passing along reconnaissance material at the checkpoint into East Berlin. She would transcribe the tapes one at a time and give me the Word files. I was reminded of Charles Dickens writing a weekly serial, handing one chapter at a time so the transcriptionist could see what happens next.

Soon enough, I was producing far too much for one person to handle, so I hired a second typist. I burned them both out, even gave one carpal-tunnel syndrome from trying to keep up with me. I scared off one potential typist with a single Dune tape; she simply couldn't handle the strange science fiction setting and vocabulary!

With microcassettes, I was forced to use only local people because I didn't want to package and mail the cassettes. I had no way to back them up, so if my tapes got lost or damaged in the mail, then I would lose all my writing permanently. Finally, with the advent of digital recorders I was able to email audio files.

I started using a typist in the Los Angeles area, who was already a big fan of my work. She also worked as a research assistant for game shows, and she enjoyed fact-checking my work. She would transcribe each chapter and add helpful comments, point out inconsistencies or continuity errors, correct me when I made a mistake (particularly about horses), even mention when she found a section boring. It was like having a typist and a first reader all in one! She also once remarked, after receiving a series of files I had recorded while mountain climbing, that with all my deep panting breaths, she felt like she was transcribing an obscene phone call!

But this was only a part-time gig for her, and I'm a prolific writer, especially once I learned how to use dictation. On average I write half a million words a year. Now I primarily use a typing service, WeScribe-It.com, which has enough people to keep up with my output.

Each day after I've dictated my chapters, I download the files from my recorder and submit them as a new project to the typing service. I get the transcribed files back in a day or two, depending on the workload of the typists. The cost is about a penny a word, so a 5,000-word short story would cost me $50 to transcribe. For a beginning writer, this cost might not be feasible. I can certainly sell a short story for more than fifty dollars.

In the next section, Martin will talk about transcription software. Since I've been doing this for a very long time, I have always preferred an actual human typist. A human has many advantages, in that he or she already knows how to put in the proper punctuation and to add paragraphs, which means I can be in the zone and write my story without jerking myself out of it to specify every comma, open quote or close quote. I would have to search out homonyms for when the software used "they're" instead of "there." Using dictation software may be cheaper, but it will take you, the writer, a lot more time to clean up the files. (Caveat: voice-recognition software gets remarkably better, year after year.)

Think what happens when I dictate the following, exactly:

"Hello Kevin great day for dictating isn't it a little windy for me because I'm going out on the trail but since you're in the car driving it shouldn't affect you at all on the other hand I'm doing a medieval fantasy in the forest so the rushing pine trees add atmospheric detail well if your typist can understand the words I'll steer clear hey can you give me a ride to the trailhead I would but I have writing to do in the car I won't interrupt, I promise yes you will no I won't I would never keep a writer from his daily wordcount."

My human typist, however, hears the changes in inflection in my voice and knows there are two people talking. She will automatically put in the paragraphs, the punctuation, the quote marks, without me saying any of it and disrupting my creative flow. Here's what will come back from the transcriptionist:

"Hello, Kevin. Great day for dictating isn't it?"

"A little windy for me, because I'm going out on the trail, but since you're in the car driving, it shouldn't affect you at all. On the other hand, I'm doing a medieval fantasy in the forest, so the rushing pine trees add atmospheric detail."

"Well, if your typist can understand the words! I'll steer clear."

"Hey, can you give me a ride to the trailhead?"

"I would, but I have writing to do in the car."

"I won't interrupt, I promise——"

"Yes, you will."

"No, I won't! I would never keep a writer from his daily wordcount."

The sheer time I save in cleanup allows me to write a lot more (though, I do still have to clean up, tighten, polish, and fill in the blanks a lot).

I wrote to the manager of WeScribeIt.com to get a little more background on the service. He replied, "We're a smaller company started in 2008. We use US typists and try to have competitive rates. We're able to give personal service because we have people that care about the client. So, normally someone signs up and once that process is complete, they log in and upload an audio file to be transcribed. Depending on if it's a rush or not, and our workload at the time, is when one of our typists begins to transcribe the audio for the client, so that's where the turnaround fluctuates. Once the transcript is completed, it's uploaded to WeScribeIt, and the client gets an email informing them that their Word doc is complete."

At present, I am their only fiction author client (though you might want to check them out). "We have a few financial advisors, sometimes interviews for movies with actors, and a few movie narrations (I assume for closed captioning). No real one specialty."

If you search under "Transcription services" you will find many options. While I'm only familiar with the one I use, a few things you should keep in mind is to make sure the service uses native English speakers (rather than farming the job overseas) and make sure they actually use a human typist, rather than just running your file through voice-recognition software, which will likely be fraught with errors (and if they are using software, as Martin will describe in the next section, you may as well be doing it yourself for free.)

Using a human typist, particularly someone you know, did raise one particular drawback I would not have encountered using dictation software. One of my typists was a shy, straightlaced older woman, and I sent her a chapter that had a fairly intense and graphic sex scene. That was a bit embarrassing!

But she was a professional, and even commented at the end, "Oooooh, spicy!"

We just didn't talk about it afterward.

—KJA

Once in a while I have a file (perhaps an older one) that's too noisy or otherwise not suited to transcription software. So I occasionally use a transcription service as well. And I have some advice when it comes to selecting a service: look for one that charges per word, not per minute. (And I found per minute or per hour to be more common than per word, with a dollar per minute being common.) My dictation rate can vary widely. My absolute best was 5,000 words in 50 minutes, or 100 words per minute.

At a dollar per minute, that works out to a penny per word, just like Kevin describes. But on an average day, I dictate closer to 50 words per minute; and on a day where I'm thinking a lot, trying to puzzle out a problem, I dictate only 25 words per minute. Suddenly a dollar per minute is 4 cents per word! A per-minute charge is just too risky for me.

—MLS

Using Transcription Software

The Case for Software:

Why would you choose transcription software over a good transcription service? For me there was one compelling reason: money.

When I started dictating, I did all of my own transcription, by hand. The benefit of this is that I had complete control, and I had the advantage of knowing what I meant. My transcriptions were essentially perfect. But! They took too long. I'm not a fast typist: five to six pages per hour (though I can type for many hours when I have to), or roughly twenty-five words per minute. That's actually about the speed that I speak, if I have pauses to think; but transcription is about more than just typing. Often you have to back up to make sure you heard correctly. (Professional transcriptionists use special foot pedals so they can control the playback while keeping their hands on the keyboard.) My experience was that it took me three hours to transcribe one hour of dictation. Instead of saving me time, manual transcription was costing me far more time. (But if you're a much faster typist, it might work for you.)

Next, I tried a transcription service. I started with a private individual, a kind and conscientious person —who could not possibly keep up with my rate of production, not if she wanted to keep her day job. (And I couldn't pay her enough to quit!) So I found a commercial service, one that charged a very reasonable rate: 1.25 cents per word. On the one hand, any story I sell to a professional science fiction market earns at least 8 cents per word, so that sounds like a good investment; but on the other hand, I can't count on selling every word I write. (I'm not Kevin, after all.) I'm very grateful to sell about 20 percent of what I write; and suddenly the transcription costs are a much larger share of overall income. And those costs must be paid in advance, while sales can take months or years. My first novel cost just over a thousand dollars to transcribe, and then took almost a year to sell. So I had a significant up-front investment.

So reluctantly but inevitably, I looked into dictation software. For reasons discussed below, I settled on Dragon NaturallySpeaking Professional. The list price is $300, but it is often for sale at half that price, or even less. But even at $300, look at my math. I dictate at least 3,000 words a day, sometimes as many as 10,000. If I pay a service 1.25 cents per word, that's at least $37.50 per day. The money I saved paid for Dragon in under two weeks.

There are other solutions. Some are relatively free. Some have a monthly fee. Each has its strengths and weaknesses; but the better options are all less costly than a transcription service.

But not necessarily better ...

The Case Against *Software:*

If I reach a point in my career where I can reliably sell a higher percentage of the words I write, I'll definitely reconsider using a dictation service. At least today, transcription software is simplistic and literal-minded, whereas a human transcriptionist is flexible and adaptable. Humans learn. They solve problems. They ask questions when they don't understand. Over time, you can develop a relationship with them, where they understand your particular style and habits.

There are also limitations in current transcription technology. I hesitate to get into technical details, because software changes so quickly; but in general, software does not cope well with noisy recordings. I have a story that I dictated during a long trip through a thunderstorm. No software I tried could pick out the words amid the noise of that recording, but human transcriptionists did! Were they perfect? No, but there were no more than around ten errors per page. The best software had ten errors per sentence. The software results were unusable, and the human transcription was more than good enough for a first draft. In this case, human transcription was worth every penny. (Well, every penny-and-a-quarter ...)

Transcription software also has difficulty dealing with accents and dialects. It can be trained (as discussed below), but it still has limits. Dragon NaturallySpeaking 15 supports an impressive eighty-six languages/dialects across sixty countries; but that's still a small subset of all possible dialects. For English, it supports Australian, British, Indian, Singapore, South African, and USA; but in reality, each of those has many regional dialects, some barely recognizable to speakers of other dialects. And what about ESL (English as a Second Language) speakers? Kevin's friend and coauthor Sarah A. Hoyt speaks English fluently but with a heavy Portuguese accent that has defeated every software transcription tool she's tried.

So transcription software (sadly) won't work for everyone.

I'm still a strong believer in good transcription software; but I go back to my earlier discussion of use cases. Software is a great solution for my specific use cases; it may not be the best choice for yours.

Setting Expectations:

As I discussed above, human transcriptionists are adaptable, while software is less so. So I find it is helpful to set your expectations for the software.

My personal expectations can be summarized as "A clean, useful first draft." I don't expect perfection— it's not as if my prose is perfect anyway—just a highly accurate capture of my words. I plan to edit the results anyway, so a small rate of errors is just part of the process.

But you may have other use cases. If you're dictating email or messages that you intend to send soon after dictation, your tolerance for errors may be lower. Or perhaps like Sir Terry Pratchett, you have difficulty using a keyboard, and you need transcription that is much closer to finished copy.

There are ways to improve the accuracy of your finished text. First, your choice of tool can affect the accuracy. There are two broad categories of transcription tools: local solutions, which perform the transcription inside your computer (including Dragon NaturallySpeaking); and web-based solutions, which send the transcription to a web server on the internet to do the transcription work (which includes all phone-based tools, plus some computer tools).

The advantage of a web-based solution is raw power: the transcription servers are more powerful than almost any desktop or laptop computer, and power improves accuracy. While I appreciate the power of a web-based solution, I prefer a local solution because I am often disconnected from the internet.

(Some users may also have privacy concerns with web-based solutions, since your entire audio is sent to a computer that's out of your control. The audio may be archived for training and auditing purposes. It may also be subject to search by governments and other third parties. This should not be construed as legal advice, but it is a reason why some users prefer a local solution.)

Second, your software is only as good as the audio you feed it, which depends on the environment where you dictate and the microphone you use. The accuracy of Dragon NaturallySpeaking for recordings in my noisy car using a low-end microphone is so poor as to be unusable; but a better microphone makes the results better than I hoped. In a low-noise environment, my Sennheiser ME-3 II microphone produces nearly perfect transcriptions.

Third, many software tools allow you to provide a list of known words, so that the software may more easily recognize them. This is particularly helpful for names, especially the made-up names and terms in fantasy and science fiction stories. Dragon Naturally-Speaking even allows you to train it how to pronounce new words.

Fourth, some software tools allow you to train them to your voice, usually by reading some long text passage so that they can compare your pronunciation to some standard. Training used to be mandatory in older versions of Dragon NaturallySpeaking (and other dictation tools). Many users are impatient to start dictating (and the software and hardware have gotten much better), so today training is optional; but it's still highly recommended if you want the best accuracy.

One caveat, though, is that you should train in the same environment where you will dictate, using the same equipment. (Dragon even allows you to set up different user profiles for different environments.) If you dictate while driving or hiking, this can be a problem: you have to read your screen and speak into your computer while in motion. This is an unacceptable safety hazard. (I don't have to tell you not to do this, do I?) I'm not sure how you might train your software while hiking (maybe standing at a table, not moving but at least out in the open), but I do have an answer for driving: ask a friend to drive your car while you read and train. (Many thanks to my sister, Anita Buckowing, for helping me to train my Dragon!)

The fifth way to improve your accuracy with most tools is to learn to speak your punctuation. Dragon NaturallySpeaking 15 has a new feature that lets it guess where commas, periods, and question marks go from your intonation. It even makes pretty good guesses, most of the time. But you'll get better punctuation and a wider range if you learn to speak it. And before you say it: yes, I know this feels awkward. And it sounds even more awkward if someone listens to you do it.

But I'm here to tell you colon after a while comma it becomes quite natural period How long is a while question mark It took me a month or so comma and I still recall how awkward it was at first period But now dot dot dot It has become so natural to me that I fall right into it with no effort dash dash and I sometimes forget I'm doing it comma and I find myself speaking punctuation to fellow humans exclamation point New line

It really has become that easy for me, with practice. I never bother speaking quotation marks—I'm only after a good first draft, remember—and I don't worry if it's not perfect. I'm going to clean it up later anyway.

And that leads to a final way to improve the accuracy of software transcription, one I confess I'm usually too busy to practice. Use the built-in editing tools to correct your transcribed text. This allows you, like Pratchett, to "type" a document completely hands-free; but more than that, it allows the transcription software to learn from its mistakes. When you correct its misunderstanding of a word, the software revises its internal model of how you speak. The next time you speak the same word in the same way, chances are that the software will recognize it correctly. With a lot of corrections over time, the software zeroes in on your precise speech patterns.

But how do you correct the transcription? Through speech, of course! Tools that support correction and training usually have phrases you can use while dictating to correct the text. (This means you have to read the text as you're dictating. So now you know why I don't use this feature.) Here are a few examples of Dragon's correction phrases:

• Scratch that: Erase the last thing you spoke. (This one I can usually use while driving, since I can remember my last few sentences.) Also Delete that and Undo that.

• Select next character: Select the next character in the text. You can also select a number of characters, and you can select forward or backward.

• Select next word: Like characters, you can select multiple words, forward or backward.

• Select next line: Or multiple lines, forward or backward.

• Select next paragraph: Or ...

• Unselect that: to clear your selection.

• Select some word: selects the next instance of the specified word.

• Select some word to other word: selects all text between and including two specified words.

Once you have selected text, you can dictate replacement text. But more than that, you can say Correct that to correct your most recent text, or Correct some word to other word to open a correction dialog box that will let Dragon show you the words it heard and also other words it might have heard. You can use your voice to select the right interpretation, or to dictate replacement text. When you use the correction dialog, Dragon will remember your choices, and it will try to do better next time.

The details of editing are both complex and specific to your specific tool. If I tried to cover them all, I would essentially be retyping many pages of online help here—and only the ones for your tool would matter to you. So for more details, refer to your user manual.

Selected Transcription Tools:

This is a partial list of transcription software tools. Many other options are available, particularly web-based solutions. Furthermore, computers are constantly getting faster and more powerful, and software gets better. So consider this list a snapshot at this point in time. It should be the start of your research, not the endpoint.

• Dragon NaturallySpeaking: One of the oldest

and most capable local transcription tools, currently at version 15. I prefer the Professional version because it will transcribe recorded audio files. (The less expensive Home edition can only transcribe while you're speaking.) The accuracy is excellent, and it has top-notch editing and training support as described above. The list price is a one-time fee of $300, but you can often find it on sale for $150 or less. In my opinion, it easily pays for itself. From Nuance (nuance.com). Available for Windows computers.

[Note: a MAJOR drawback with Dragon Naturally-Speaking is that they recently stopped supporting Mac OS. This seems incomprehensible since so many writers in particular use Apple computers. The only workaround is to run Windows on the Mac, which is clumsy at best. This makes Dragon NaturallySpeaking a non-starter for me and virtually all Mac users. —KJA]

• Dragon Anywhere: This is a web-based tool from Nuance, the makers of Dragon, available for iOS (iPhone) and Android. It supports many of the editing features of Dragon NaturallySpeaking. I found the accuracy to be excellent, and it's a viable solution for those (unlike me) who have a reliable internet connection wherever they dictate. The price starts around $15 per month, with a discount for yearly subscriptions.

• iPhone/Mac Dictation: iPhone/Mac users are well familiar with Siri, the voice-controlled user assistant built into iOS. But there's more to voice on the iPhone: on the on-screen keyboard, you'll find a microphone button that allows you to speak text into any document or field on your phone. That includes Pages or whatever text editor you might use. This is web-based, so the accuracy is high, as long as you have an internet connection. It doesn't have the editing features of Dragon Anywhere, but it's free!

• Android Dictation: I can't speak for the transcription quality of Android dictation, since I'm not an Android user, but it's a web-based solution similar in capabilities to iPhone dictation.

• Google Docs: On the Chrome browser, Google Docs adds a Dictate button for a web-based transcription tool.

• Microsoft Word: It's not something that most users notice, but recent versions of Microsoft Word have a Dictate button to enable a local transcription tool. It supports editing commands similar to Dragon Naturally Speaking.

Putting the Software to Use:

In Chapter 7, I described my process of dictating while I drive. Now I'll describe the rest of my process: transcription using Dragon NaturallySpeaking.

Kevin discussed transcription services earlier in this chapter. I'm a big fan of good services. Occasionally, I have recordings that are too noisy for transcription software. Before I got my high-end microphone, road noise and traffic noise and the passing wind often made my recordings unintelligible to software, but perfectly intelligible to human beings. (There are still at least a few things humans do better than the machines.) But today I work primarily with Dragon.

My dictation day starts with my hour of commute in the morning where I dictate 1,500 words. Then when I get out of work, I sit back down in the Aldrin, seat myself in the story by listening to my last five minutes of the morning's dictation, and start back up again, dictating and driving. When I get home at night, I have two hours of audio that I copy from my recorder onto the computer, then I run it through the transcription software. It takes a few minutes—I really haven't measured, but it's less than five—to transcribe an hour of audio. (This is why I no longer do my own transcription by hand. Five minutes vs. three hours? No contest.)

After I transcribe each file, I copy it into a folder called Listened to. Why do I save the file? The honest answer is that I'm a packrat. I have a hard time throwing anything away. I tell myself that the transcription might be wrong, and I might want to go back and listen to it and fix what I meant to say versus what the transcription heard. And who knows? Maybe one day the recordings will end up in my archives. (Note to future archivists: please ignore the language that sometimes happens when the traffic around me is full of idiots.)

Dragon transcribes an audio file into an RTF document and opens it in a little application called DragonPad. That application has a lot of editing features, as I discussed above, but I don't use any of them. All I do is copy and paste into my Word document, and then transcribe the next file.

Then it's time to edit! But this isn't a book on editing, so you're on your own there. I clean up, add punctuation or fix it where needed, correct names, etc. And I reorganize as necessary, pick out the best versions of different sentences, and generally produce a second draft that is ready to send to my first readers.

This is a process I built up over years. I didn't do this right away, so don't worry if it seems like that's too easy and you could never do it. It takes practice. You'll get better.

—MLS

Afterword

While we were writing the first draft of this book (which took us about a week, working sporadically), Kevin received the following serendipitous letter.

I wanted to drop you a line of thanks for your book *Million Dollar Productivity* for the impact it's had on my writing career. I lead a very busy life with three kids, a full-time job, and a number of other "life" factors that often make it hard to write. I've always carved out time for writing every day, be it during breaks, heading to work a half-hour early, or while waiting to pick up the kids from school, but I've never managed more than maybe 500-1,000 words a day this way. After reading your book, it clicked that I'd never considered dictation as an option for writing stories. I have an hour commute to work and with the help of dictation through Google Docs, I've managed to increase my output to 3k or more words per day. I'm finishing the first drafts of my stories so very quickly by adding in my commute time to my daily writing routine. It might seem odd to receive a thank you for something so obvious, but reading your book has made a huge impact in my career. Thanks a ton, Kevin.—Eric S. Fomley

See, we're not the only ones who do it.

A few days later, when Kevin posted an announcement on Facebook that we were writing *On Being a Dictator*, he received a message from another writer, Jason J. Willis:

"I just did a pair of long brainstorming sessions just last night with my Olympus. When I got back, I plugged it into its base and Dragon turned it into text (quite well, by the way). Dictation not only seems to make my mind work drastically better, but it's great for my health and doesn't even feel like exercise."

You're not just talking to yourself. You're working. You're writing. You're exercising. You're getting inspired!

By adding dictation to your writer's toolbox, you will find the method to be liberating and, once you become fully accustomed to it, dictating will feel even more natural than typing on a keyboard.

Even if you just use dictation for brainstorming your ideas, concocting character backgrounds, or working out plot snags, you will find it is an effective tool to unlock your creativity. We aren't surprised to read numerous studies that have found that physical movement and a change of scenery inspire creativity.

Kevin has written countless chapters about alien worlds and incredible fantasy adventures while walking through mountains, forests, deserts, or high-walled canyons. When you surround yourself with vivid details and sensory input, it naturally comes through in your writing.

Martin has transformed his daily commute into productive worktime, increasing his output substantially. Kevin also dictates while driving, using even short drives to write blogs, introductions, and brief articles (including much of this book).

Even though we do most of our writing by dictation, it is just another method. We also write on the keyboard, or even with pen and notepad if necessary. "A writer writes!" as the great Billy Crystal said in the perfect writer's movie, *Throw Momma from the Train*.

In our case, a writer talks, and the typist transcribes.

Stay in shape. Get inspired. Be productive.

And be a dictator!

Appendix:
STAKE by Kevin J. Anderson

CHAPTER 1
Notes, Dictated Draft, Final

This is the first chapter for my vampire/serial-killer thriller **Stake**, *from audible.com, a tense novel about a murderer who truly believes in vampires and thinks he is saving the world by hunting down suspected vampires.*

I wrote my detailed outline, 53 chapters, worked through several iterations with my audible.com editor, and then I was ready to write.

My brief notes for Chapter 1:

1. Colorado Springs: Majestic Pike's Peak dusted with an early coating of snow, aspens in the Front Range turning gold, clear and intense blue sky. A perfect day for killing vampires.

It is broad daylight, and most of the apartment building is empty. People have gone to work, kids have rushed off to school. The place has an aura of brooding quiet, almost abandoned, like many residential areas in the middle of the work day. But one of the apartments is dark, and all the windows are covered with thick drapes. A hand-lettered sign on the door says QUIET—DO NOT DISTURB.

Exactly the indications SIMON HELSING has come to expect.

Disguised as a plumber, carrying a tool kit, he sneaks up to the door of the darkened dwelling, then works quietly to break in. Inside, he sprinkles himself with Holy Water, dangles a cross and garlic around his neck, getting ready for battle. Then he creeps into the bedroom where he finds a man lying deeply asleep. MARK STALLINGS. The uniform shirt from the man's job at an all-night convenience store lies draped on a chair. Never seen in daylight, signs are obvious for those who know what to look for. Helsing has a complete file on him, did his research, surveillance, made himself absolutely sure.

Helsing (which we learn later is not his real name, but one he has adopted) pulls on rubber gloves. He removes a mallet and a wooden stake from his toolbox, positions it over the chest of the sleeping man. "May God have mercy on your soul," he mutters, just loudly enough to wake the victim. The victim doesn't even have time to cry out before Simon lifts the mallet and drives the stake through his heart, then strikes a second time for good measure....

I printed that and took the slip of paper with me when I went out to dictate the chapter. What follows is the transcription of my dictation, word for word, exactly as it came back from the typist.

If you want to hear my actual audio file, as I composed the prose off the top of my head, I have made it available at https://myaudiosample.com/dictator.

CHAPTER 1 (from transcriptionist)
Colorado Springs, Colorado
September

A light dusting of early season snow covered the gray shoulders of Pike's Peak that rose majestically above the city. Aspens turned gold in the rugged Front Range like a splash of honey signaling the turn of the seasons. Despite the bit in the air the sky was deep blue over the city, brisk and crystal clear. The sun shone down.

The conditions were perfect for killing a vampire.

In broad daylight in the early afternoon the apartment complex was mostly quiet, the majority of people at work except for a handful of busy preschool kids playing on the courtyard swing set or riding plastic Big Wheels along the sidewalk while their mothers, probably military wives, watched the kids and chatted with one another or played games on their phones. They didn't notice him. Simon Helsing knew how to be invisible using a camouflage of "normalness," similar techniques that vampires had used for centuries. Even though at this time of day the vampires powers would be at their lowest. He knew from past mistakes that bystanders could be as big of a threat as the vampires themselves. He wore a plumber's shirt and a Broncos cap over his long brown hair. He carried a toolkit which carried the tools – the weapons – that he needed, not the tools a plumber would use. He had a set of fake work orders and heh walked with the casual confidence that would tell any observer that he was supposed to be there. He climbed the concrete steps to the second floor, glanced again at the paperwork as if to double check although he knew full well that the creature's lair was in apartment 220. Helsing went up to the door and pretended a polite knock making little noise. He knew that at the height of day when the vampire was in the deepest stupor of sleep possibly having fed well the night before would not be awakened by a simple knock. But the job was risky enough as it was and he didn't like to take chances. Waiting patiently in case anyone was watching and receiving no answer to his imaginary knock he removed his lock picks as if the apartment building management had given him access. Simon Helsing wasn't his actual name but he had adopted it a few years ago when he embraced his new mission. It fit him like a calfskin glove. He had an online identity and an off the radar presence in Colorado Springs. He knew who he was but he felt it important to maintain a quiet profile so he could do his work even though the Community offered him some support and Lucius shared the same mission. Helsing was alone. After he opened the door of apartment 220 he entered the darkened please sure he smelled shadows and blood. All the drapes were drawn, heavy opaque drapes rather than the standard dishrags usually found over the windows in cheap apartments like this. The man inside had also added night blocking window shades to make sure no sunlight got in during the day. He closed the door behind him and froze sensing the threat. He could always sense the brooding evil. The room was neat, austere with basic furniture that had no doubt come with the apartment. No pictures on the walls, very little clutter that would have been apparent in any normal place where a human lived. Helsing had done his research carefully, had surveilled the target. He had no doubts. He set the toolkit down on a folded grocery store flyer and other junk mail on the coffee table surface. He made no sound except for the slightest muffled click as he opened the latch, lifted the metal lid and withdrew his heavy wooden mallet and the pointed pinewood stake which he had sharpened himself.

He still heard no noise except for the faint ticking of the clock built into the stove in the small kitchen. He looked through the living room, saw the door to the bathroom, then another door mostly closed. The bedroom. Where the vampire slept during the hours of sunlight. Mark Stallings worked as a nighttime clerk in a convenience store on North Academy. He had filled the nightshift for three years straight never once, as far as Helsing could tell, filling in during daylight hours. Stallings was only seen in the safety of darkness. Helsing had done his research. More telling, according to public access records that Helsing had diligently searched Stallings was a ghost before he had moved to Colorado Springs. No previous addresses, no tax forms filed, not even a prior driver's license in any other state that Helsing could find. No family – no siblings, no parents, no wives, ex or otherwise. He was alone, a cipher living without notice…feeding without being caught. Over the past three years a total of four tenants in the apartment building had mysteriously vanished simply moving away without any notice, without any forwarding address. Helsing believed their bodies were discretely hidden somewhere, maybe some of the unidentified corpses the community found and dealt with burning them before they could turn. [Insert above. A hand-lettered sign on an index card permanently taped to the apartment door said QUIET – DO NOT DISTURB.] He drew a deep breath strengthening his resolve preparing for his terrible work. At the bottom of the toolkit he had a sealed jar filled with holy water he had taken from one of the many Catholic churches in the Springs. Like some kind of sacred cologne he dabbed it on his face, on his neck, then rubbed more on his neck just in case. Then he slipped a chain with a prominent cross over his head displaying it at the base of his throat. He wasn't sure exactly how effective any of the religious trappings were but he knew that such a rich trove of folklore had to have some basis in fact. A talisman was a talisman and he wouldn't discount any protection it might afford. He was ready taking the mallet and stake he crept into the vampire's bedroom. Stallings laid sound asleep in the darkened room. The uniform shirt from the convenience store hung on a chair in front of a cheap build-it-yourself computer desk. A clothes hamper sat next to the computer desk with as many clothes strewn on the floor around it as inside it. Helsing could smell the animal odor of the creature, possibly even sour blood from a recent victim. Stallings was an indistinct silhouette on the bed surrounded by a rumpled sheet. He was utterly quiet, not snoring. Vampires needed to breathe less than normal humans. He had a beard and reddish brown hair now matted with sleep. Helsing had seen photos, had discretely taken them himself during his surveillance. There was no doubt in his mind that he didn't make mistakes. He lay with his head turned on the pillow, eyes closed in sleep but on his back exposing his chest. Good. Helsing didn't like the added risk if he needed to roll him over. [Insert earlier: He pulled on a pair of rubber gloves tugging them tight far up on his wrists. He would not dare let the tainted blood infect him and often these killings were a terrible mess.] He crept to the bed and loomed over the vampire. Stallings didn't stir. He carefully positioned the pointed tip of the pine stake over the man's chest directly above the sternum. Stallings didn't stir. In his left hand he gripped the handle of the mallet, positioned it just above the top of the stake, then raised it like a carpenter about to pound a nail into a two-by-four. He let the point just touch the vampire's skin.

"May God have mercy on your soul," Helsing whispered, then lifted his arm high.

Feeling the wooden point Stallings started, blinked his eyes and turned his head. "What," he managed to say before Helsing drove the mallet down with all his might with a loud crack. The point plunged through the breastbone, pounded down into the vampire's heart with a spurt of hot blood. Even before the victim could twist and jitter, as they always did, he pounded a second time for good measure through the heart and pinning him to the bed.

END CHAPTER

That's pretty clean, but it needs some polishing. After I dictated the entire novel, I went back and started editing. **Stake** *eventually went through seven drafts until the editor and I considered it ready for prime time. Here is the final, final draft of the first chapter. As you can see, it didn't change all that much:*

CHAPTER 1 (final edit)

A dusting of early-season snow covered the gray shoulders of Pike's Peak, and aspens splashed gold along the Front Range to the west of Colorado Springs. The clear blue sky was bursting with sunlight.

Perfect conditions for killing a vampire.

Just after noon, the Serenity Hedge apartments felt subdued, with most people off at their day jobs. Preschoolers played on the courtyard swing set or rode plastic Big Wheels along the sidewalk, while their mothers chatted.

No one noticed him as he approached with practiced nonchalance.

Simon Helsing knew how to stay invisible. For centuries, vampires had used similar techniques to move unseen through everyday society. At this time of day, a vampire's powers would be at their lowest point, but nosy observers could also pose a great threat.

Helsing wore a gray plumber's shirt and a Colorado Avalanche cap over his long brown hair. His battered metal toolkit held weapons rather than plumbing tools. Carrying fake work orders he had produced on a public printer down at the library, he walked with a casual confidence that told the world he was supposed to be there.

Helsing climbed the concrete exterior steps to the second floor of apartments, glanced again at the paperwork as if to double check the address, though he knew full well that the creature's lair was in #220. A hand-lettered index card permanently taped to the door said Quiet! Do Not Disturb.

He pantomimed a polite knock, but made no noise. At the height of day the vampire would be in a deep sleep, likely having fed well the night before, and a simple knock wouldn't wake him. But Helsing didn't like to take chances. The job was risky enough as it was.

After waiting an appropriate time for an answer, he got out his picks and smoothly unlocked the door, as if the building manager had given him access. He slipped into a dark, sinister apartment that smelled of shadows and blood. He closed the door behind him, no longer worried about being seen, but he was in danger nevertheless. He froze for a moment, assessing the threat inside. He could sense the brooding evil. Yes, this was the place.

He had adopted the name "Simon Helsing" when he embraced his new mission, and it fit him like a calf-skin glove. He lived entirely off the radar in Colorado Springs; it was important to maintain a quiet profile so he could do his work. Even though the members of the Bastion offered him support, and their leader Lucius shared the same mission of saving the human race, Helsing did his bloody work alone.

After hunting the lampir—the Bosnian word for vampire—in secret for years, he had decided to change tactics. No longer did it serve his purpose, or humanity's, to hide his crusade. People needed to know that real monsters lived unnoticed among them.

He waited for his eyes to adjust to the apartment's dark interior. The curtains were made of a heavy opaque fabric, a significant upgrade from the flimsy dishrags usually found in cheap dwellings. The inhabitant had added light-blocking window shades to prevent any purifying sunlight from seeping through.

The front room held minimal furniture—sofa, chair, coffee table, end table, lamp—austere basics that had probably come with the apartment. No pictures on the walls, little of the clutter he would have found in any normal human home.

The place was silent as a tomb except for the faint ticking of the stove clock in the small kitchen. Helsing remained still as he peered through the gloom, discerning the door to a hall bathroom and a second mostly closed door—the room where the vampire slept during daylight.

Before moving forward, he rested his toolkit on the sofa and opened the latch with only a muffled click. He raised the metal lid and withdrew a mallet and the wooden stake he had sharpened.

Helsing had surveilled the target, studied his background. Mark Stallings worked as a nighttime clerk in a convenience store on North Academy Drive. He had filled the night shift for three years straight and never once, as far as Helsing could tell, worked during daylight hours. More telling, according to public records "Stallings" had not existed before he moved to Colorado Springs. No previous addresses, no tax returns, not even a driver's license in any other state. No siblings, no parents, no wives, ex or otherwise. He was alone, a cipher who drew no attention to himself so he could feed without being caught.

Over the past three years, four separate tenants in the Serenity Hedge apartments had mysteriously vanished without giving notice or leaving a forwarding address. Helsing was convinced that Stallings had killed them and discreetly disposed of their bodies. Or maybe the victims were among the unidentified corpses burned by members of the Bastion to prevent them from turning into lampir themselves.

Drawing a deep breath, Helsing strengthened his resolve to move forward with his terrible work. From the kit he removed a plastic bottle of holy water filled in St. Mary's Cathedral downtown. As if it were sacred cologne, he dabbed the moisture on his face and neck, then slipped the cross on its chain over his head and adjusted it. He wasn't sure how effective such religious trappings were, and he was not religious himself, but centuries of folklore had to have some basis in fact. The peasants near Sarajevo knew what worked, and he would accept any protection the cross might provide.

He pulled on a pair of latex gloves and crept to the vampire's lair with the mallet and stake in hand.

As soon as he pushed open the bedroom door, he could smell the creature's animal odor, possibly even rank blood from a recent victim. Stallings lay flat on his back, sound asleep in the darkened room, an indistinct silhouette under a rumpled sheet. The convenience store uniform shirt hung on a chair in front of a cheap build-it-yourself desk. Clothes lay strewn around a hamper in the corner.

Stallings was utterly quiet, not snoring, sleeping as if dead. Vampires needed to breathe less than normal humans. The creature had a beard and reddish brown hair matted with sleep. He wore dark flannel pajamas with the shirt unbuttoned, conveniently exposing his chest. His head was turned on the pillow, eyes closed.

Three silent steps took Helsing to the side of the

bed, where he loomed over Stallings. The lampir didn't stir.

Helsing positioned the tip of the stake directly above the sternum, and gripped the mallet like a carpenter about to pound a nail into a two-by-four. He let the sharpened point just touch the vampire's skin. "You'll never hurt anyone else," he whispered.

When the wooden point touched his chest, Stallings started, and blinked his eyes. "What—?"

Helsing raised the mallet high and brought it down using all his strength. The point punched through the breastbone and pierced the vampire's heart with a spurt of hot blood.

Even before the monster began to twist and jitter, as they always did, Helsing pounded a second time with a loud crack, driving the wood all the way through the back. The stake pinned the body to the bed so that it could never again rise from the dead.

Disclaimer and Credits

The authors and publisher have strived to be as accurate and complete as possible in creating the Million Dollar Writing series. We don't believe in magical outcomes from our advice. We do believe in hard work and helping others. The advice in our Million Dollar Writing series is intended to offer new tools and approaches to writing. We make no guarantees about any individual's ability to get results or earn money with our ideas, information, tools or strategies. We do want to help by giving great content, direction and strategies to move writers forward faster. Nothing in this book is a promise or guarantee of future book sales or earnings. Any numbers referenced in this series are estimates or projections, and should not be considered exact, actual or as a promise of potential earnings. All numbers are for the purpose of illustration. The sole purpose of these materials is to educate and entertain. Any perceived slights to specific organizations or individuals are unintentional. The publisher and authors are not engaged in rendering legal, accounting, financial, or other professional services. If legal or expert assistance is required, the services of a competent professional should be sought.

Dictaphone is a registered trademark of Dictaphone Corporation.

Sennheiser is a registered trademark of Sennheiser Electronic K.G.

Olympus is a registered trademark of Olympus Corporation.

Jeep is a registered trademark of Chrysler Group LLC.

NaturallySpeaking and Nuance are registered trademarks of Nuance Communications, Inc.

Kindle is a registered trademark of Amazon Technologies, Inc.

iPhone is a registered trademark of Apple Inc.

Android and Google are registered trademarks of Google LLC.

Windows and Microsoft are registered trademarks of Microsoft Corporation.

About the Authors

Kevin J. Anderson has published 160 books, 56 of which have been national or international bestsellers. He has written numerous novels in the Star Wars, X-Files, Dune, and DC Comics universes, as well as unique steampunk fantasy novels *Clockwork Angels* and *Clockwork Lives*, written with legendary rock drummer from Rush, Neil Peart. His original works include the Saga of Seven Suns series, the Terra Incognita fantasy trilogy, the Saga of Shadows trilogy, and *Spine of the Dragon*. He has edited numerous anthologies, written comics and games, and the lyrics to two rock CDs. Anderson and his wife Rebecca Moesta are the publishers of WordFire Press. He is Director of the Publishing MA Program at Western Colorado University.

Martin L. Shoemaker is a programmer who writes on the side … or maybe it's the other way around. He told stories to imaginary friends and learned to type on his brother's manual typewriter even though he couldn't reach the keys. (He still types with the keyboard in his lap today.) He couldn't imagine any career but writing fiction … until his algebra teacher said, "This is a program. You should write one of these."

Fast forward 30 years of programming, writing, and teaching. He was named an MVP by Microsoft for his work with the developer community. He is an avid role-playing gamemaster, but that didn't satisfy his storytelling urge. He wrote, but he never submitted until his brother-in-law read a chapter and said, "That's not a chapter. That's a story. Send it in." It won second place in the Baen Memorial Writing Contest and earned him lunch with Buzz Aldrin. Programming never did that!

Martin hasn't stopped writing (or programming) since. His novella "Murder on the Aldrin Express" was reprinted in *The Year's Best Science Fiction: Thirty-First Annual Collection* and in *Year's Top Short SF Novels 4*. His work has appeared in *Analog, Galaxy's Edge, Digital Science Fiction, Forever Magazine, Writers of the Future 31, Year's Best Military and Adventure SF 4, Avatar Dreams*, and select service garages worldwide. He received the Washington Science Fiction Association Small Press Award for his Clarkesworld story "Today I Am Paul," which also was nominated for a Nebula Award and appeared in four *Year's Best* anthologies and eight international editions. The story continues in *Today I Am Carey*, published by Baen Books in March 2019. Another novel, *The Last Dance*, will be published by 47North in Fall 2019.

Learn more at Shoemaker.Space.

You Might Also Enjoy

Million Dollar Productivity
Million Dollar Professionalism
Worldbuilding: From Small Towns to Entire Universes
Writing as a Team Sport

Our list of other WordFire Press authors and titles is always growing. To find out more and to see our selection of titles, visit us at:
wordfirepress.com

Made in the USA
Middletown, DE
12 January 2020